PROTEST KNITS

HERBERT PRESS

LONDON · OXFORD · NEW YORK · NEW DELHI · SYDNEY

Herbert Press
An imprint of Bloomsbury Publishing Plc

50 Bedford Square
London
WC1B 3DP
UK

1385 Broadway
New York
NY 10018
USA

www.bloomsbury.com

BLOOMSBURY and HERBERT PRESS are trade marks of Bloomsbury Publishing Plc

First published in Great Britain 2017

© Bloomsbury Publishing plc
Created for Bloomsbury by Plum5 Ltd
Written by Geraldine Warner
Technical Editor Gwendolyn Wagner-Adair (Petitchoufleur Knits)

British Library Cataloguing-in-Publication Data
A catalogue record for this book is available from the British Library.

Library of Congress Cataloguing-in-Publication data has been applied for.

ISBN: HB: 978-1-9122-1700-7

ePub: 978-1-9122-1701-4

ePDF: 978-1-912217-02-1

2 4 6 8 10 9 7 5 3 1

Printed and bound in Barcelona, Spain, by Tallers Gràfics Soler

To find out more about our authors and books visit www.bloomsbury.com. Here you will find extracts, author interviews, details of forthcoming events and the option to sign up for our newsletters.

CONTENTS

On January 20th 2017, Donald John Trump was inaugurated as the 45th President of the United States. Four months later, the world's first protest from space was staged. Yup, you read that right – the Autonomous Space Agency Network (a community promoting open-source, DIY space exploration) flew a message addressed to Trump reading "LOOK AT THAT YOU SON OF A BITCH" and got it up to 90,000 feet above the earth's surface attached to a weather balloon.

Take a look around at what's going on – how did we get here? We're witnessing and taking part in the highest number of protests this century has seen so far, and feelings are running so high that protestors are searching for ever more innovative ways to make their voices heard. When democracy and human rights are threatened, every voice counts and we have to use all the tools we can lay our hands on – not everyone can get hold of a handy weather balloon, but we protestors are a notoriously resourceful bunch; how about channelling your anger by grabbing your your needles and yarn to fight the good fight?

This collection of 17 knitting and crochet projects should get your activist juices flowing, all capturing the spirit of protest and revolution, mixed in with a liberal dose of the humour in evidence at so many recent protest marches worldwide. Craft itself is undergoing something of a revolution and ties into a grassroots folk tradition – the materials are cheap, readily available and get the message across. You could even start up a protest knit community and work on projects together while you hotly debate the issues at hand.

The book includes something for every occasion, ranging from the quick and simple (labelled Easy), to items with a longer-term view (labelled Difficult). Even the difficult ones aren't that hard, although they might call on your colourwork skills.

I came here to knit hats and punch nazis and I'm all outta yarn

A Short History

Knitting and Protests

Fun fact: knitting as a hobby is a relatively recent activity, although traditionally it already comes with some baggage. For the last 100 years it has brought with it images of comfort and home-making, and is seen as a genteel pastime enabling women to feel they're doing something useful and productive with their spare time.

It has had its moments however: in *No Idle Hands*, Anne McDonald looks at the important role that knitters and female crafters had to play in the American War of Independence through the creation of garments and home furnishings to help break UK dependence. Back in old Blighty, from the Boer War onwards, women were urged to knit for the men fighting abroad, while the Second World War gave the activity a sense of innovation as yarn was rationed and clothing was unravelled to be recrafted into new items.

As it became cheaper to buy clothing instead of making it, and lack of spare time rendered the hobby a less useful activity for busy women, knitting faded from popularity along with sewing and other textile crafts. In addition to economic practicalities, the image of women sitting at home knitting did not fit in with the modern feminist movement's challenge to traditional female constructs. Happily, the recent post-technological craft revolution has seen a new wave of makers coming through who want to subvert the conservative image presented by knitting and to take it out of the realms of the passive into a more active arena.

In 2005, a Houston-based group of knitting

individuals formed the group Knitta Please. With names inspired by hip-hop stars (LoopDogg, SonOfAStitch, The Knotorious N.I.T.), and their method of "tagging" their work, they conjured a more challenging attitude. They took to the urban streets with their own brand of knitted graffiti, decorating lamp-posts, railings, fire hydrants, and anything else they considered would benefit from a bit of woolly beautification.

This fun, edgy version of knitting took off worldwide, and hundreds of cities and towns saw increasingly ambitious knitted graffiti springing up in the streets. The term "yarn-bombing" was born, lending the craft a more aggressive slant.

Fast-forward a decade and sadly, women once again feel they need to challenge their role in society. As the liberal western world faces a battle with the political right, we are motivated to provide a loud reminder of how hard we have fought to gain some gender equilibrium. The beauty of this method of subversion is that instead of ignoring its feminine roots, it both uses and challenges them at the same time. On the one hand, a woman knitting? Great, she knows her place! On the other, an activist woman using the craft to knit protest slogans? Wait, what's wrong with this picture?!

The Pussy Hat is the perfect embodiment of just that. It first came to the attention of the media at the beginning of 2017, along with a leaked audio-clip of the recently-inaugurated POTUS Donald Trump discussing women: "When you're a star they let you do it. Grab them by the pussy. You can do anything." As a result, the pink Pussy Hat was born – an instant, easy to make visual statement which, when worn en masse, has enormous impact. Dare you to grab this pussy! Keen not to be lumped in with this image of outdated sexism, men joined in the protest and wore their own versions.

This new chapter in the rich histories of both knitting and protest movements sees a perfect blend of activism and grassroots craft – viva protest knits!

I can't believe we're still protesting this shit

The book supposes you have a basic knowledge of knitting and crochet, but there are some specific techniques and references used in this book. Here's a guide to some of the more common ones featured throughout.

KNITTING TECHNIQUES

Duplicate Stitch (Swiss Darning) (used for Open-Top Mittens, p.58, and Fingerless Gloves, p.42)

1. Thread a blunt darning needle with yarn and secure at back of fabric.
2. Bring needle from back to front of work at base of stitch to be covered and draw yarn through. Insert needle behind the 2 loops of stitch above from right to left and draw yarn through. Insert needle into base of stitch again and bring up at base of next stitch to be covered. Draw yarn through loosely so stitches lie on top of knitting. Continue in this way until entire motif is embroidered.

Grafting (Kitchener Stitch) (used for Anarchist Socks, p.18)

Grafting (also known as weaving or Kitchener stitch) is used when joining two pieces of knitting together for a seamless join (the wool needle is used to mimic the knit stitch for a seamless join). In order to join the pieces together, the stitches to be grafted need to remain on the needles (the same number of sts are required on each needle). The pieces are grafted from Right to Left.

The following example uses St-st as the primary stitch.

1. Insert sewing needle knit-wise through first st on front knitting needle, draw yarn through and sl the st off the knitting needle.
2. Insert sewing needle purl-wise through next st on front knitting needle, draw yarn through but leave the st on the needle.
3. Insert sewing needle purl-wise through the first st on back knitting needle, draw yarn through and sl the st off.
4. Insert sewing needle knit-wise through the next st on back knitting needle, leaving the st on the needle.

Rep Steps 1-4 until all sts have been worked.

I-cord (used for Brain Hat, p.38)

A knitted tubular cord, created with two dpns:

1. Cast on 3 or 4 sts according to pattern instructions. Knit 1 row. Do not turn.
2. Slide sts along the dpn back to right-hand tip of needle.
3. Swap needle to left hand ready for the next row. Knit the sts, pulling yarn tight across the back of the sts. Do not turn.

Rep Steps 2-3 until cord is desired length.
Cut yarn, thread tail through sts and pull tight.

Moss Stitch (US Seed Stitch)

Moss stitch is used often throughout these patterns as it makes for a firmer fabric and neat edges, useful in smaller items. Depending on the number of sts called for in the pattern, moss stitch is worked as follows:

Odd number of sts:

Row 1: K1, p1; rep to last st, k1.
Rep for desired number of rows.

Even number of sts:

Row 1: K1, p1; rep to end.
Row 2: P1, k1; rep to end.
Rep these 2 rows for desired number of rows.

Stocking Stitch (or Stockinette)

One of the most basic stitches, this creates a tight-knit fabric, and is worked back and forth as follows:

Row 1 (RS): Knit.
Row 2 (WS): Purl.

Note: When working Stocking stitch in the round (rather than back and forth in rows), knit every round. (This is because you are always working on the right side of the fabric.)

Tension/Gauge

This is the section that most people skip over but which is actually very important, particularly when knitted items will be worn and fit is important (i.e., the projects for gloves and scarves in this book). You may be confident that your own tension is usually pretty close to the mark when you've knit from patterns in the past, but you should ALWAYS make sure that it matches the guidelines in individual patterns.

Each pattern has a tension/gauge guide; the guidelines are measured over 10cm (4") and expect you to knit a swatch measuring the same. The instructions will also tell you which stitch was used to work up the swatch where more than one stitch is used in the pattern. Where the tension (gauge) is negligible (for smaller objects, crochet flowers etc) or tension has been measured after washing and blocking, this is noted at the beginning of the pattern.

Wrap & Turn (w&t) (used in Anarchist Socks, p.18 and Flask holder, p.50)

Some of the patterns in this book use short rows or partial knitting as a shaping method. The work is turned before the row is completed, and worked over several rows; this creates extra fabric in one area of the knitting. When you turn the work, a hole appears when all the stitches are worked over again. Use the Wrap & Turn technique as follows to hide this hole (in the instructions it is abbreviated to w&t):

Row 1 (RS): Knit to the turning point (w&t). Wrap the next st as follows: slip the st purl-wise onto the right-hand needle, bring the yarn forward between the needles to front of work. Slip the st back onto the left-hand needle, take the yarn back between the needles to back of work, then turn the work so that the WS is facing.

Row 2 (WS): Purl the required number of sts. Wrap the next st as follows: slip the st purl-wise onto the right-hand needle, take the yarn back between the needles to back of work. Slip the st back onto the left-hand needle, bring the yarn forward between the needles to the front of the work, then turn the work so that the RS is facing.

Each wrapped stitch will have a strand of yarn laying across its base. When the short row section is completed and you work across all the stitches, pick up the strand from the bottom so it is sitting on your needle, then purl the strand together with the wrapped st.

FINISHING

Each pattern has its own directions concerning the construction of the project, but we leave the specific methods chosen up to you. Having said that, here are some issues you might like to consider:

Casting On & Off

There are many different casting-on and off techniques so please feel free to use your preferred method – for simplicity's sake we recommend a standard cable cast-on.

1. Create a slip-knot.
2. Insert the right needle knitwise into the st on the left needle.
3. Wrap the yarn round the right needle as if to knit.
4. Draw the yarn through the first st to make a new st, but instead slip the new st to the left needle.
5. Insert the right needle between the two sts on the left needle.
6. Wrap the yarn around the right needle as if to knit and pull the yarn through to make a new st.
7. Slip the new st to the left needle. Rep Steps 5–7 until required number of sts has been cast-on.

French Knot (used in Womb, p.22)

Thread a sewing needle with one strand of yarn, or more for bigger knots.

1. Bring needle up at desired place and wrap thread twice around needle.
2. Insert needle close to where it came up, holding wrapped thread taut.
3. Pass needle through the fabric, leaving the knot on the surface.

Do not pull thread too tight or the knot may disappear to the back of the fabric.

Back Stitch

1. Pin the two pieces of knitting together.
2. Working from right to left, starting where you would like the seam to begin, push the needle through both layers of knitting from top to bottom and come out approx 1cm (½") to the left.
3. Insert the needle back into the knitting to the right of the needle, approximately 0.5cm (¼") to the right of where the original stitch came out.
4. Bring the needle back through the layers from bottom to top 1cm (½") to the left of the stitch.
5. Continue until the end of the seam.

Overstitch (or whip stitch)

1. Bring your needle up through both pieces of fabric from bottom to top and pull through.
2. Pass the yarn over the seam and repeat Step 1 a little further along from the last stitch.
3. Continue until the end of the seam.

Basic Techniques
Crochet

CROCHET TECHNIQUES

Basic stitches

There are 5 crochet projects in this book, most of which use very basic crochet sts. There is a difference in crochet terminology between the UK and US (see Abbreviations below). The instructions in this book use UK terminology as default, with US terms in brackets (i.e., Work 5 dc (sc) – this is the same st with different names). See Abbreviations (p.14) for differences in US and UK terminology.

Here is a brief guide to the crochet stitches used in this book.

Chain stitch: The foundation of crochet work. Make a sl st and place over hook. With the yarn in position, pass the hook under the yarn held in the other hand and catch yarn with hook. Draw yarn through loop on hook. Rep this action until chain is the desired length.

Double crochet (single crochet): Begin with 1 chain for turning (see Turning Chains), then put the hook into the second stitch to left of hook, yarn over hook, draw through a loop (2 loops on hook), yarn over hook and draw through 2 loops on hook (1 loop remains on hook). Continue working each stitch this way omitting the turning chain until the beginning of the next row.

Half treble (half double crochet): Begin with 2 chains for turning (see Turning Chains), then yarn over hook, put hook into third stitch to left of hook, yarn over hook and draw through a loop (3 loops on hook), yarn over hook, draw yarn through all loops on hook (1 loop remains on hook). Continue working each stitch this way omitting the 2 turning chains until the beginning of the next row.

Treble (Half double crochet): Begin with 3 chains for turning (see Turning Chains), then yarn over hook, put hook into fourth stitch to left of hook, yarn over hook and draw through a loop (3 loops on hook), yarn over hook and draw through 2 loops on hook, yarn over hook and draw yarn through remaining 2 loops (1 loop remains on hook). Continue working each stitch this way omitting the 3 turning chains until the beginning of the next row.

Turning Chains

Each crochet project will include instructions for how many turning chains to make at the beginning of each row. If in doubt, the rule of thumb is as follows:

dc (sc) = 1 turning chain
htr (hdc) = 2 turning chains
tr (dc) = 3 turning chains

Changing Colour

When changing colour, do so on the last stitch of the old colour – so when working in dc (sc) stitches you would insert hook into next stitch, yarn over with the old colour, pull through and yarn over with the new colour before pulling this through the 2 loops on your hook.

When changing colours, hold the secondary colour behind your work as you go so that you can easily switch between the two and not end up with too many loose tails.

Decrease

The decreases are only worked at the beginning or end of the row in this book, as follows: work the turning chain to count as the first stitch in the usual way, miss the second stitch from the hook, work in pattern to the last 2 stitches, miss the next stitch and work the last stitch.

Magic Ring (also known as Magic Loop or Circle) used in Voodoo Trump, p.70

When you are working in the round, the Magic Ring is a great way to create a tight foundation circle without any gaps. Work as follows:

1. To start a Magic Ring, don't make a slipknot. Instead, make a loop with the yarn, leaving a tail around 10cm (4") long. Make sure the tail end is hanging down.

2. Now insert your hook into the loop, from front to back. Wrap the working yarn around the hook anti-clockwise and pull the yarn through the Magic Ring.

3. Now work your stitches into the Magic Ring, making sure all the stitches are worked over both the loop itself and the tail end (so two strands of yarn).

4. Once you've worked the number of stitches you need, simply pull the tail end of the yarn to draw up the ring – magic!

5. Close rnd with a slip stitch as usual.

Abbreviations

KNITTING

"	inch(es)
approx	approximately
cm	centimetres
cont	continue
dec	decrease
dpn(s)	double-pointed needles
garter-st	garter st (knit every row)
g	grams
inc	increase
k	knit
kfb	knit into front & back of next stitch (increases 1 stitch)
kfbf	knit into front, back and front again of next stitch (increases 2 stitches)
k2tog	knit two together
m	metres
m1L	make a stitch by inserting your left needle into the loop lying in front of the next stitch from front to back, then knit into the back of the stitch. Creates a "\\" shape
m1R	make a stitch by inserting your left needle into the loop lying in front of the next stitch from back to front then knit into the front of the stitch (knitwise). Creates a "/" shape.
MC	main colour
mm	millimetres
oz	ounces
p	purl
p2tog	purl two together

patt	pattern
PM	place marker
psso	pass slipped stitch over
rem	remaining
rep	repeat
rnd(s)	round(s)
RS	right side
skpo	slip one, knit one, pass the slipped stitch over
sm	slip marker
st(s)	stitch(es)
St-st	stocking stitch
w&t	wrap and turn (see Basic Techniques, p.8)
WS	wrong side
yds	yards

CROCHET

ch	chain
dc (sc)	double crochet (single crochet in US)
htr (hdc)	half treble (half double crochet in US)
sl st	slip stitch
tr (dc)	treble (double crochet in US)

WEIGHT CONVERSION

50g = 1¾oz

100g = 3½oz

KNITTING PATTERNS

Shy Anarchist Socks

For timid activists

Let's face it, we all have days when we want to play it down a bit, when our yang is… Well you get the message. If you find yourself in a situation where you don't feel like shouting about your beliefs but still want to do your bit, then these socks are just for you. You can walk around all day in a seemingly innocent pair of stripy footwear until you hitch up your trouser leg, et voila! Your true feelings are miraculously revealed.

Knitted in the round, using short rows for the heel shaping and stranded colourwork for the anarchist motif, these socks knit up pretty quickly.

DIFFICULTY LEVEL: HARD

MATERIALS

Regia 4-ply (75% Wool/25% Nylon, 50g/210m/229yds) as follows:

- 1 x 50g balls in shade #2054 (Red) (A)
- 1 x 50g balls in shade #2080 (Super White) (B)
- 1 x 50g ball in shade #1980 (Greyblue) (C)
- 4 x 2.75mm (US 2) dpns
- 4 x 3mm (US 3) dpns

TENSION/GAUGE

30 sts and 40 rows = 10cm (4") over St-st

SIZE

Cuff to heel: 23cm (9")

Foot circumference: 21.5cm (8.5")

Foot length: adapt according to instructions

Question authority

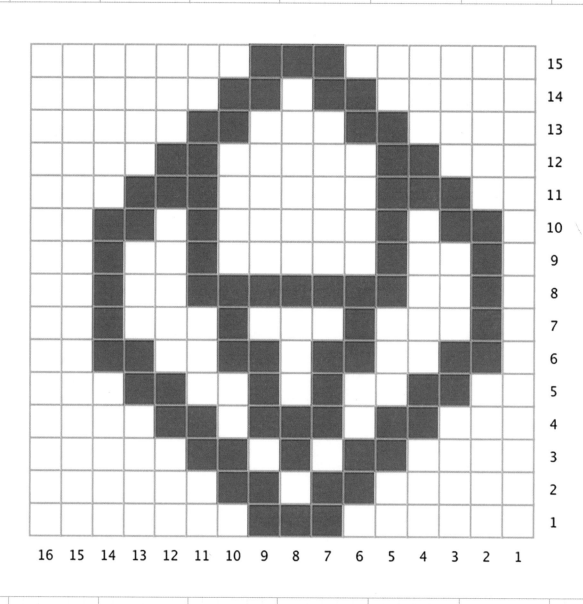

INSTRUCTIONS

Socks (Make 2)

With 2.75mm dpns and A, cast on 64 sts. Distribute the sts as follows: 22/22/20. Join in to work in the rnd, ensuring there are no twists and PM. Work 3.75cm (1½") in (k1, p1) rib. Do not break yarn. Change to 3mm dpns. Change to B, work 2 rows in St-st, then work as follows: **Next 15 rnds:** Using A and B, work Chart to end of rnd (four reps around). Change to B, k 2 rnds, then work in striped St-st patt below as follows until sock measures 17.5cm (7") from cast-on edge or desired length. **Next 5 rnds:** K in C. **Next 5 rnds:** K in B.

Divide for Heel and Instep

Change to A, k32 sts. Sl these 32 sts onto same dpn and cont in A on these sts only for heel.

Heel

Row 1 (WS): Sl1, p to end of row, turn. **Row 2:** Sl1, k30, w&t. **Row 3:** Sl1, p29, w&t. **Row 4 (RS):** Sl1, k to 1 st before last w&t, w&t. **Row 5 (WS):** Sl1, p to 1 st before last w&t, w&t. Rep these two rows until you have 12 sts between the w&ts. **Row 22 (RS):** Sl1, k12, pick and work wrap with its companion st, turn. **Row 23:** Sl1, p12, pick up and work wrap with its companion st, turn. Cont to work 1 further st on each row (remembering to work wraps with their companion st to prevent holes) until you have worked across all 32 sts.

You will now be working around all sts again. Distribute sts over 3 dpns (22/22/20). Cont in stripe patt until foot measures approx 3.75cm (1½") less than desired sock foot length.

Shape Toe

Break off B and C and cont in A. **Rnd 1:** (K32, PM) twice. **Rnd 2**: (K1, skpo, k to 3 sts before marker, k2tog, k1, sm) twice. (4 sts dec) **Rnd 3:** (K to marker, sm) twice. **Rnds 4-13:** Rep Rnds 2-3 five more times. (40 sts) **Rnd 14-17:**

Rep Rnd 2 four times. (24 sts) Sl first 12 sts onto one needle and rem 12 sts onto a second needle. Break yarn, leaving a 38cm (15") tail. Graft sts together using Kitchener st.

FINISHING

Darn in ends.

Knitted Womb

A womb with a view

Problem: too many men having a say in what women do with their own bodies. Be part of the solution: get busy and send this quick-to-knit uterus to those unenlightened lawmakers. If you get enough of your friends to knit and send, those guys will soon get the idea that women mean business. Alternatively, sew a brooch fitting to the back and wear it with pride.

The womb is very quick and easy to knit up in the round – we've given ours a happy face, but you could make yours angry or sad, depending on your own mood.

DIFFICULTY LEVEL: EASY

MATERIALS

■ 1 x 50g ball King Cole Merino Blend DK (100% Wool, 50g/112m/122 yds) in shade #787 (Fuchsia)
Small amount of black yarn to embroider face
Small amount of toy stuffing
4 x 4mm (US 6) dpns
1 x 3cm (1¼") metal brooch back
Darning needle (for embroidering face)

TENSION/GAUGE

21 sts and 26 rows = 10cm (4") over St-st

SIZE

6.5cm (2½") (w) x 7.5cm (3") (h)

INSTRUCTIONS

Cast on 8 sts and distribute over 3 dpns as follows: 3/2/3. **Rnds 1-2:** K 2 rnds. **Rnd3:** (K2tog, k2) twice. (6 sts) **Rnds 4-5:** K. **Rnd 6:** (K2tog, k1) twice. (4 sts) **Rnd 7:** K. **Rnd 8:** Kfb; rep to end. (8 sts)

Rnd 9: K. **Rnd 10:** (K1, kfb); rep to end. (12 sts) **Rnd 11:** K. **Rnd 12:** (Kfb twice, k1); rep to end. (20 sts) **Rnds 13-14:** K. **Rnd 15:** (Kfb twice, k3); rep to end. (28 sts) **Rnds 16-18:** K. **Rnd 19:** (Kfb twice, k5); rep to end. (36 sts) **Rnds 20-22:** K. **Rnd 23:** (K2tog twice, k5); rep to end. (28 sts) **Rnd 24:** (K2tog twice, k3); rep to end. (20 sts) **Rnd 25:** (K2tog twice, k1); rep to end. (12 sts) Stuff. **Rnd 26:** (K2tog); rep to end. (6 sts) **Rnd 27:** (K2tog); rep to end. (3 sts) Break yarn leaving a long tail. Thread tail through rem sts, draw tight and secure on inside.

Fallopian Tubes (Make 2)

Using 2 dpns, cast on 4 sts. Work as for i-cord (see p.8) until piece measures 7.5cm (3").
Next rnd: (K2tog) twice, break yarn leaving a long tail (approx 24cm (10")) and thread tail through rem sts using a darning needle. Secure, then make approx 5 or 6 small loops at the end of the tube. Secure and darn in ends.

FINISHING

Position and pin the tubes at each side of the Womb near the top, using the pictures as a guide. Sew in place.

To embroider face (optional)

Using black yarn and a darning needle, work two French knots for eyes, then make a loop next to the eye for the eyelashes and secure yarn. Cut the loops in half to make eyelashes. Work a mouth using backstitch.

Balaclava & Beard

Good for bad hair days

Some protesters are wary of the powers that be tracking them down but those plastic Guy Fawkes masks can be a bit chilly. For a warmer anonymous protest try this chic balaclava (beard optional, naturally). They'll be all the rage in Hoxton. Added bonus: the combo keeps you ridiculously warm on cold days and is also great for bad hair days. Or bad beard days.

This is a quick, fairly easy knit in 2x2 rib and St-st. The optional beard is attached using press studs.

DIFFICULTY LEVEL: MEDIUM

MATERIALS

Adriafil Regina (100% wool/50g/125m/136 yds)
as follows:

■ 3 x 50g balls in shade #16 (Brown) (MC)
■ 1 x 50g ball in shade #92 (Camel) (CC)
4mm (US 6) circular needle (40cm (16") long)
1 pair 4mm (US 6) needles
St-holder
2 x press studs

TENSION/GAUGE

21 sts and 26 rows = 10cm (4") over St-st

SIZE

To fit medium-size head: 53.5cm–56cm (21"–22")
with 5cm (2") positive ease after blocking

Be the change

INSTRUCTIONS

Balaclava

Using 4mm circular needle and MC, cast on 120 sts. Join to work in the rnd, ensuring there are no twists and PM. Work in (k2, p2) rib until work measures 12cm (4¾"). Turn at end of last rnd; piece will now be worked back and forth in rows instead of rnds.

Row 1 (WS): P86, slip rem 34 sts onto a st-holder for chin, turn. **Rows 2-61:** Work 60 rows in St-st, always slipping first st of every row purl-wise. **Row 62:** K58, sl1, k1, psso, turn. (57 sts) **Row 63:** P31, p2tog, turn. (56 sts) **Row 64:** K31, sl1, k1, psso, turn. (55 sts) **Row 65:** P31, p2tog, turn. (54 sts) Rep last 2 rows until 32sts rem. **Next row:** (K2tog) twice, (k1, k2tog) 7 times, k1, (k2tog) 3 times. (20 sts) Work rib edging as follows: pick up and k31 sts down side of balaclava, work 34 chin sts from st-holder in (k2, p2) rib, pick up and k 31 sts up the other side of balaclava, then k7 sts from beginning of needle. PM. Work 9 rnds in (k2, p2) rib. Cast off in rib.

Beard

Using 4mm needles and CC, cast on 3 sts. Row 1 (RS): Kfb, moss-st to last st, kfb. (5 sts) Rep Row 1 until 17 sts. **Next row:** Work in moss-st. **Next row:** Kfb, moss-st to last st, kfb. (19 sts) Rep last two rows to 33 sts. **Next row:** Cont in patt as set, moss-st 9 sts, cast off 15 sts, moss-st 9 sts. Place last 9 sts onto st-holder and return to first set of 9 sts. Work 3 rows in moss-st and break yarn. With WS facing, re-join yarn to 9 sts on st-holder and work 3 rows in moss-st. **Next row (RS):** Cont in patt as set, moss-st 9 sts, cast on 15 sts, moss-st 9 sts. (33 sts) Work 6 rows in moss-st as set. **Next 2 rows:** Cast off 1 st at each end. (29 sts) Cast off.

Moustache

Using 4mm needles and CC, cast on 1 st. **Row 1 (RS):** Kfbf. (3 sts) **Row 2:** Work in moss-st. **Row 3:** Kfb, moss-st to last st, kfb. (5 sts) Rep last 2 rows until 11 sts. Cont in moss-st until piece measures 6.5cm (2½"). **Next row:** K2tog twice, moss-st 3 sts, k2tog twice. (7 sts) **Next row:** K2tog, moss-st 3 sts, k2tog. (5 sts) **Next row:** K2tog, moss-st 1 st, k2tog. (3 sts) **Next row:** Kfb, moss-st 1 st, kfb. (5 sts) **Next row:** Kfb, moss-st 3 sts, kfb. (7 sts) **Next row:** Kfb twice, moss-st 3 sts, kfb twice. (11 sts) Cont in moss-st until piece measures 13cm (5") from cast-on edge. **Next row:** K2tog, moss-st to last 2 sts, k2tog. (9 sts) **Next row:** Work in moss-st. Rep last 2 rows until 3 sts rem. K3tog. Break yarn, draw yarn through st.

FINISHING

Turn hat inside out so that WS is facing. Press lightly using a warm iron over a damp cloth. Press WS of Beard and Moustache in the same way. Place the Moustache centrally over the top edge of the Beard and sew into place. Darn in ends. Sew press studs to either side of the balaclava opening, and sew matching press stud halves on the WS of beard so that it lines up with your nose and mouth. Rock the look.

Smart is the new pretty

Pussy Hat

Reclaim the pussy!

Reclaim the pussy! It's hard to imagine a time when the pussy hat wasn't a thing, but grudge-thanks to a hot mic throwaway comment by Agent Orange himself and hell, we've turned the pussy on its head (so to speak) ... The insult is now a word of feminine power, and what better way to show it? If you can't make it to a protest, show your solidarity by pulling on one of these feline numbers and turn the streets into a sea of pink.

This simple pattern knits up nice and quick in DK on circular needles, making it easy to knit more than one for your non-knitting pussy pals.

DIFFICULTY LEVEL: EASY

MATERIALS

King Cole Merino Blend DK (100% Wool, 50g/112m/122yds) as follows:

- 2 x 50g balls in shade #907 (Raspberry) (A)
- 1 x 50g ball in shade #1532 (Pale Pink) (B)

4mm (US 6) circular needle (40cm (16") long)

TENSION/GAUGE

21 sts and 26 rows = 10cm (4") over St-st after blocking

SIZE

To fit medium-size head: 53.5cm–56cm (21"–22") with 2.5cm (1") negative ease

INSTRUCTIONS

With circular needle and A, cast on 110 sts. Join to work in the rnd, ensuring there are no twists and PM. Work in (k1, p1) rib until piece measures 5cm (2"). Now work in St-st (k all sts) as follows: Work 6 rnds in A. Change to B, work 6 rnds. Break B and cont to work in A until piece measures 18cm (7"). Cast off.

FINISHING

Turn work inside out so that WS is facing. Press lightly using a warm iron over a damp cloth. Sew the top seam.

Ears (rep for each corner): With RS facing, measure 7.5cm (3") away from the corner along both the top and side of the hat and mark with pins, then seam along the diagonal line between the pins. This forms the triangle for the ear. Darn in ends.

Our pussies are not up for grabs

Button Badges

Right on the button

Ah, the button badge; old friend to many a seasoned protester wanting to make a statement. Back in the 60s, you couldn't move without bumping into a longhair sporting a peace badge, and what did the punk movement turn to during the 70s? You guessed it… The history of the badge goes back further still to the 19th century, so keep it up to date with these knitted symbols of resistance… Long live the button badge!

Simple, quick knitting at its best.

DIFFICULTY LEVEL: EASY

MATERIALS

Patons Fairytale Fab 4-ply (100% Acrylic, 50g/184m/201yds) as follows:

☐ 1 x 50g ball in shade #1001 (White) (A)

■ 1 x 50g ball in shade #1099 (Black) (B)

1 pair 3.25mm (US 3) needles

Small amount of toy stuffing

7.5cm (3") blank button badge

Darning needle (for Power Fist detail)

2 x 8.25cm (3¼") diameter circles cut out of thick card

TENSION/GAUGE

30 sts and 40 rows = 10cm (4") over St-st

SIZE

9cm (3½") (d)

Don't hate, appreciate

protest knits **35**

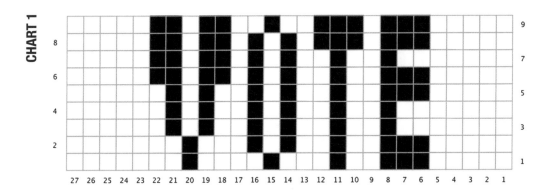

CHART 1

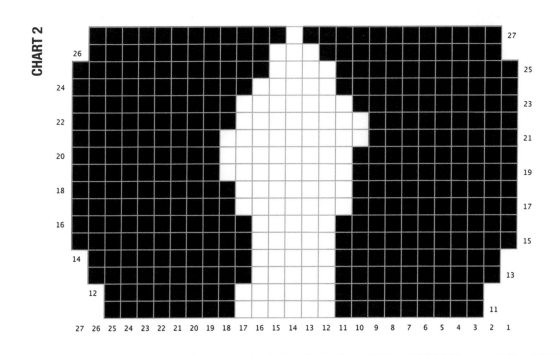

CHART 2

INSTRUCTIONS

Vote Badge

With A, cast on 7 sts and proceed in St-st. **Row 1 (RS):** K. **Rows 2-3:** Cast on 2 sts, work to end. (11 sts) **Rows 4-5:** Inc 1 st at each end of row. (15 sts) **Rows 6-7:** Cast on 2 sts, work to end. (19 sts) **Row 8:** Inc 1 st at each end of row. (21 sts) **Row 9:** K. **Row 10:** Inc 1 st at each end of row. (23 sts) **Rows 11-12:** Work even in St-st without increasing. **Row 13:** Inc 1 st at each end of row. (25 sts) **Row 14:** P. **Row 15:** Inc 1 st at each end of row. (27 sts) **Row 16:** P. **Rows 17-25:** Using A and B, work Chart 1 to end. **Row 26:** Dec 1 st at each end of row. (25 sts) Row 27: Work even in St-st without decreasing. **Row 28:** Dec 1 st at each end of row. (23 sts) **Rows 29-30:** Work even in St-st without decreasing. **Rows 31:** Dec 1 st at each end of row. (21 sts) **Row 32:** Work even without decreasing. **Row 33:** Dec 1 st at each end of row. (19 sts) **Rows 34-35:** Cast off 2 sts, work to end. (15 sts) **Rows 36-37:** Dec 1 st at each end of row. (11 sts) **Rows 38-39:** Cast off 2 sts at beg of row, work to end. (7 sts) **Row 40:** P. Cast off, leaving a long tail measuring approx 20cm (8").

Power Fist Badge

With B, work exactly as for Vote Badge to Row 10, then cont to work shaping, with A and B work Chart 2 over Rows 11 – 27. Cont to work Rows 28-40 as per Vote Badge.

Love peace,
hate pieces

FINISHING

For the Power Fist Badge only:

Create the outline of the fingers and the fist with A using back stitch.

For both badges:

Sew a running stitch around the outside of the knitted badge but do not gather. With knitted work WS facing up, place a small amount of flattened toy stuffing over the surface, then place the cardboard circle on top of this, followed by the plastic button badge (face down). Gather the running thread so that it encompasses all the layers and forms an edge around the back of the badge. Secure the yarn and darn in ends.

Brain Hat

Use your head, dummy

Fake news this and fake news that ... you need all your wits about you to suss out the difference between truth and lies. There are a lot of wild statements being thrown around – some taking on science itself; what with climate change denial on the up and funding for scientific research on the down, get yourself along to an Earth Day Science March and join the brainiac brigade!

The hat itself is very simple, knitted in the round with coiled i-cord stitched to the surface.

DIFFICULTY LEVEL: EASY

MATERIALS

■ 3 x 50g balls King Cole Merino Blend DK (100% Wool, 50g/112m/122yds) in shade #1532 (Pale Pink)

4 x 4mm (US 6) dpns

2 x 5mm (US 8) dpns

4mm (US 6) circular needle (40cm (16") long)

TENSION/GAUGE

21 sts and 26 rows = 10cm (4") over St-st after blocking

SIZE

To fit medium-size head: 53.5cm–56cm (21"–22") with 2.5cm (1") negative ease

NOTES

When shaping crown, switch to dpns when sts no longer fit around circular needle.

INSTRUCTIONS

Using 4mm circular needle, cast on 110 sts. Join to work in the rnd, ensuring there are no twists and PM. Work 5cm (2") in (k1, p1) rib. Now cont in St-st (knit all sts) until piece measures 14cm (5½") from cast-on edge.

Shape Crown: Next row: (K3, k2tog); rep to end. (88 sts) **Next row:** K. **Next row:** (K2, k2tog); rep to end. (66 sts) **Next row:** K. **Next row:** (K1, k2tog); rep to end. (44 sts) **Next row:** K. **Next row:** K2tog to end. (22 sts) **Next row:** K2tog to end. (11 sts) Break yarn leaving a long tail, and thread tail through rem sts. Secure.

Brain Cord (Make 2): Using two 5mm dpns, cast on 4 sts. Work as for i-cord (see Basic Techniques, p.8) until piece measures approx 381cm (150").

FINISHING

Turn main hat inside out so that WS is facing. Press lightly using a warm iron over a damp cloth. Mark the hat into two halves (left and right hemispheres) with pins or tacking, then arrange and pin the i-cords separately over each half, looping each one back on itself in an appropriate pattern to mimic the cerebral cortex. Sew i-cord onto hat to secure. Darn in ends.

Nasty Woman Mitts

Sugar and spice...

Sugar and spice and all things nice, right? Any woman who's had it up to here with the endless attempts to put her firmly back in the kitchen – instead of the voting booth (or in Hilary Clinton's case, the race for presidency) – will do everything she can to shake off those stereotypes. If that means landing up on the Cheeto-in-Chief's "nasty woman" list, then why not shout about it? Mansplainers, beware.

These mitts are knitted in the round using stranded colourwork for the main gloves with duplicate stitch lettering (added after knitting). You could even get creative and make your own message.

DIFFICULTY LEVEL: HARD

MATERIALS

King Cole Merino Blend 4-ply (100% Wool, 50g/180m/197yds) as follows:
☐ 1 x 50g ball in shade #046 (Aran) (A)
■ 1 x 50g ball in shade #048 (Black) (B)
■ 1 x 50g ball in shade #009 (Scarlet) (C)
4 x 3mm (US 3) dpns
St-holder
Locking st-marker (to mark chart placement)
Darning needle (for duplicate st lettering)

TENSION/GAUGE

32 sts and 42 rows = 10cm (4") over St-st (after blocking)

SIZE

20cm (8") circumference (measured around palm) / 23cm (9½") cast-on edge to top ribbing at base of fingers.

Nasty women keep fighting

CHART 1: RIGHT GLOVE

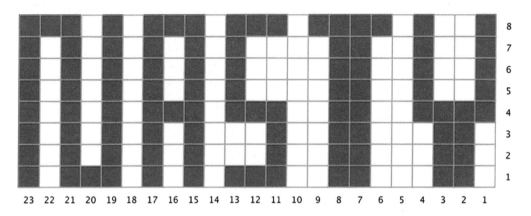

8 7 6 5 4 3 2 1

23 22 21 20 19 18 17 16 15 14 13 12 11 10 9 8 7 6 5 4 3 2 1

CHART 2: LEFT GLOVE

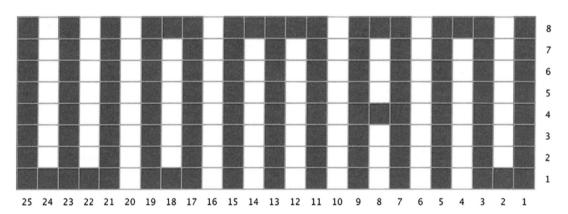

8 7 6 5 4 3 2 1

25 24 23 22 21 20 19 18 17 16 15 14 13 12 11 10 9 8 7 6 5 4 3 2 1

INSTRUCTIONS

Fingerless Mitts (make 2)

Using B, cast on 60 sts. Distribute sts evenly across 3 dpns (20 sts each). Join to work in the rnd, ensuring there are no twists and PM. **Rnds 1-3 (RS):** K. **Rnd 4:** Work the number of sts specified in the colour indicated as follows: (K2B, k2A) twice, k2B, k2C, (k2B, k2A) 7 times, k2B, k2C, (k2B, k2A) 4 times to end of rnd. Rep Rnd 4 until work measures 7.5cm (3") from cast-on edge. Break C. **Next rnd:** Using B, k to last st, kfb. (61 sts) **Next rnd:** Using B, k to end of rnd.

Start Thumb Gusset

Next rnd: Using B, k29 sts, PM, m1R, k3, m1L, k to end. (63 sts) **Next rnd:** Using B, k to end of rnd. **Next rnd:** (K1B, k1A) to marker (29 sts), sm, m1R using B, (k1A, k1B) twice, K1A, m1L using B, (k1A, k1B) to end. (65 sts) **Next rnd:** (K1A, k1B) to last st, k1A. **Next rnd:** (K1B, k1A) to last st, k1B. **Next rnd:** (K1A, k1B) to last st, k1A. **Next rnd:** Using A, k to marker, sm, m1R, k7, m1L, k to end. (67 sts) **Next rnd:** (K1B, k1A) to last st, k1B. **Next rnd:** Using A, k to end of rnd. **Next rnd:** (K1A, k1B) to last st, k1A. **Next rnd:** Using A, k to marker, sm, m1R, k9, m1L, k to end. (69 sts) **Next rnd:** Using A, k to end of rnd. **Next rnd:** (K1B, k1A) to last st, k1B. **Next rnd:** Using A, k to end of rnd. **Next rnd:** Using A, k to marker, sm, m1R, k11, m1L, k to end. (71 sts) **Next rnd:** (K1A, k1B) to last st, k1A. **Next 2 rnds:** Using A, k to end of rnd. **Next rnd:** Using A, k to marker, sm, m1R, k13, m1L, k to end. (73 sts) **Next rnd:** (K1b, k3A); rep to last st, k1A. **Next 2 rnds:** Using A, k to end of rnd. **Next rnd:** Using A, k to marker, sm, m1R, k15, m1L, k to end. (75 sts) **Next rnd:** Using A, k to end of rnd. **Next rnd:** (K1B, k5A) to last 3 sts, k3A. Break B. **Next rnd:** Using A, k to end of rnd. **Next rnd:** Using A, k to marker, sm, m1R, k17, m1L, k to end. (77 sts) **Next rnd:** Using A, k to end of rnd. **Next rnd:** Using A, k to marker, rm, place next 19 sts on st-holder for Thumb, cast on 2 sts across base of Thumb, k to end of rnd. (60 sts) **Next 14 rnds:** Using A, k to end of rnd.

Right-Hand Mitten Only

Using locking st marker, PM into st at beginning of next rnd and leave in (this will give you a marker to count in for the lettering chart).

Left-Hand Mitten Only

K30, using locking st marker, PM into st and leave in (this will give you a marker to count in for the lettering chart).

Both Mittens:

Next 4 rnds: Using A, k to end. **Next 5 rnds:** (K1B, K1A) to end of rnd. Using B, cast off in rib patt.

Thumb

Transfer 19 sts from st-holder and distribute onto 3 dpns (7/7/5). Pick up and k3 sts across cast-off edge at base of Thumb. (22 sts) PM and join to work in the rnd. **Next 2 rnds:** Using A, k to end of rnd. **Next 5 rnds:** (K1B, K1A) to end of rnd. Using B, cast off in rib patt.

FINISHING

Lettering

Place mittens so that the base of the fingers are pointing towards you. The thumbs should both be facing inwards.

Right-Hand Mitten Only

Count in 4 sts from marker and place a pin. With C and darning needle, work duplicate st lettering from Chart 1.

Left-Hand Mitten Only

Count in 3 sts from marker and place a pin. With C and darning needle, work duplicate st lettering from Chart 2. Turn mittens inside out so that WS is facing. Press lightly using a warm iron over a damp cloth. Darn in ends.

Armband

Don't sit on the fence

Wear your heart on your sleeve and speak up! This is not a time for silence and fence-sitting; the world can only be changed by people who care enough. Armbands are a great way to send a message and can be slipped on and off with no fuss. Wear this armband with attitude and tell the world everyone needs to give a damn.

The band itself is easy to knit and gives plenty of room for adjustment over bulky clothes.

DIFFICULTY LEVEL: EASY

MATERIALS

Patons Fairytale Fab 4-ply (100% Acrylic, 50g/184m/201yds) as follows:

■ 1 x 50g ball in shade #1099 (Black) (A)

□ 1 x 50g ball in shade #1022 (Sundance) (B)

1 pair 3.25mm (US 3) needles

10cm (4") strip of velcro

TENSION/GAUGE

30 sts and 40 rows = 10cm (4") over St-st (after blocking)

SIZE

49cm (19") (w) x 12cm (4½") (h) after blocking

NOTES

The lettering on the Armband is not intended to be centered – this allows for size adjustment when attaching the velcro.

INSTRUCTIONS

Using A, cast on 100 sts. K 4 rows. **Row 5 (RS):** K. **Row 6:** K4, p to last 4 sts, k4. **Row 7:** K24, using A and B work Row 1 from chart, k to end. **Row 8:** K4, p13, work Row 2 from chart, p to last 4 sts, k4. **Rows 9-29:** Cont as set, using A and B to work chart to end. **Row 30 (WS):** Rep Row 6. **Rows 31-32:** Rep Rows 5-6. **Rows 33-36:** K. Cast off.

FINISHING

Press lightly using a warm iron over a damp cloth. Darn in ends. Fit the armband around your arm so that the left-hand side overlaps (remembering to make allowances for clothing) and pin to secure. Attach velcro to each side of the armband, according to fit.

Give peace a chance

Flask Holder

Pass the tea, vicar

Want to remove the stress from a long, tricky protest situation and keep rehydrated at the same time? Passing round a hot, sugary drink should do the trick. When you're on the move and want to travel light, this handy flask holder will not only send a message, but also easily hold a half-litre thermos flask or cold bottle of water (Bonus: the insulating properties of wool mean it will even stay cooler for longer.).

A quick knit, mostly using moss-st for the main cylinder with garter-st pinwheel circles at the end (knitted on two needles).

DIFFICULTY LEVEL: MEDIUM

MATERIALS

Patons Wool DK (100% Wool, 50g/125m/136yds) as follows:

■ 1 x 50g ball in shade #171 (Olive) (A)

□ 1 x 50g ball in shade #174 (Mustard) (B)

4mm (US 6) needles

22.5cm (9") strip of velcro

76cm (30") x 2.5cm (1") wide canvas webbing (for strap)

2 x 2.5cm (1") D rings (to attach strap to holder)

1 x 2.5cm (1") slider (to adjust strap)

TENSION/GAUGE

31 sts and 38 rows = 10cm (4") over moss-st (after blocking)

SIZE

11cm (4½") (d) x 30cm (12") (l)

INSTRUCTIONS

Main Cylinder

Using A, cast on 66 sts. Work in moss-st until piece measures 14cm (5½"). **Next row:** Work 5 sts moss-st, k56, work 5 sts moss-st. **Next row:** Work 5 sts moss-st, p56, work 5 sts moss-st. **Next row (RS):** Using A, work 5 sts moss-st, k5, using A and B k46 sts following Row 1 of chart, using A, k5, work 5 sts moss-st. **Next row:** Using A, work 5 sts moss-st, p5, p46 sts following Row 2 of chart, using A, p5, work 5 sts moss-st. Cont in this way until all 16 rows of chart are complete. **Next row:** Work 5 sts moss-st, k56, work 5 sts moss-st. **Next row:** Work 5 sts moss-st, p56, work 5 sts moss-st. Work in moss-st until piece measures 33cm (13") from cast-on edge. Cast off.

Round Ends (make 2)

With A, cast on 10 sts. **Row 1 (WS):** K8, w&t. **Row 2 (and all RS rows):** K. **Row 3:** K6, w&t. **Row 5:** K4, w&t. **Row 7:** K2, w&t. **Row 9:** K across all sts, picking up and working wraps with their companion sts as you come to them. Change to B (but don't break A). Rows 10-19 below form a segment. ****Row 10:** Using B, sl1, k to end. **Rows 11-19:** Rep Rows 1 – 9.****** Change to A (but don't break B). Rep from segment pattern (Rows 10-19) 12 more times, alternating between A and B for each segment. (There should be a total of 14 segments in alternating colours.) Change to A, cast off.

FINISHING

For each Round Side: Sew the cast-off and cast-on edges together. Sew a running st around the centre and gather slightly to close the centre hole. Press all pieces lightly on WS using a warm iron over a damp cloth. Darn in ends. With WS facing, pin and sew the sides of Main Cylinder to the Round Ends, overlapping the cast-on and cast-off edges of the Main Cylinder to form the opening. Turn inside out so RS is facing. Attach the corresponding parts of the velcro to the cast-on and cast-off edges.

Strap

Sew a D ring to each side of the Round End near the top edge, so that the lettering motif faces outwards when you sling the holder over your shoulder. Cut the canvas webbing in half and sew a 1.25cm (½") hem at each end of both pieces to prevent fraying. Fold the end of one of the lengths around the D ring and sew to secure. Rep for the second length on the other D ring. Thread the slider onto one of the lengths and thread the other through. Adjust to preferred length. Drink to victory!

We're not nasty, we're revolting

Strike a pose and hold your scarf with pride. Well, if this humble piece of neckwear is good enough for football supporters to declare passion for their team, why shouldn't it be put to good use by ardent protestors? Yes, it might get a bit hot if you're wearing it en route on a hot day, so just stuff it in your bag and surprise everyone by hoisting it at the last minute.

Knitted back and forth using stranded colourwork, the scarf is pretty straightforward if you know your way around a colour chart, and is a great one to get your teeth into.

DIFFICULTY LEVEL: DIFFICULT

MATERIALS

Adriafil Regina (100% Wool, 50g/124m/136yds) as follows:

- 6 x 50g balls in shade #39 (Avio Blue) (A)
- 2 x 50g balls in shade #35 (Dark Orange) (B)
- 1 x 50g ball in shade #02 (White) (C)
- 1 x 50g ball in shade # 48 (Night) (D)

4mm (US 6) circular needle (150cm (60") long)

TENSION/GAUGE

22 sts and 32 rows = 10cm (4") over St-st (after blocking)

SIZE

150cm (50") (w) x 30cm (11¾") (h)

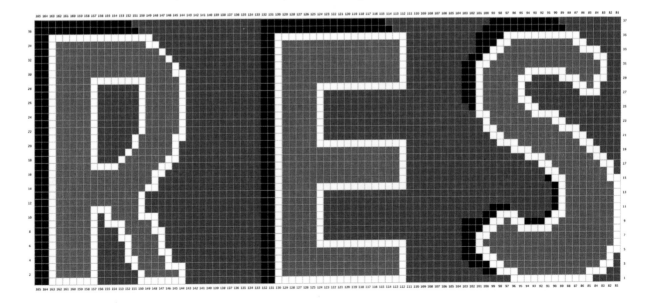

NOTES

Although this scarf is worked flat (back and forth) a circular needle is recommended due to the large number of stitches.

INSTRUCTIONS

Using 4mm circular needle and A, cast on 329 sts. Work in moss-st until piece measures 5cm (2") from cast-on edge. The middle section of the scarf is worked in St-st with 11 sts worked in moss-st at beginning and end (as set in next two rows): **Next row (RS):** Work 11 sts moss-st, k to last 11 sts, moss-st to end. **Next row:** Work 11 sts moss-st, p to last 11 sts, moss-st to end. **Next row:** Work 11 sts moss-st, k71, using A, B, C and D as indicated, work Row 1 from chart, k71, work 11 sts moss-st. **Next row:** Work 11 sts moss-st, p71, work Row 2 from chart, p71, work 11 sts moss-st. Cont as set until all 37 rows of chart are complete. Break yarns B, C and D. **Next row (WS):**

Continuing in A, work 11 sts moss-st, p to last 11 sts, work moss-st to end. **Next row:** Using A, work 11 sts moss-st, k to last 11 sts, work moss-st to end. Work in moss-st for 5cm (2"). Cast off loosely, taking care to match tension of scarf.

FINISHING

Press lightly using a warm iron over a damp cloth. Darn in ends. Take to the streets.

You are not the boss of me

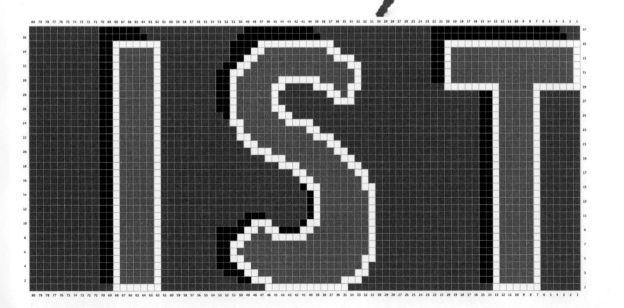

Open-Top Mittens

Bad news day

Sometimes you want a gentler type of protest, a polite, understated way of saying the situation just isn't working for you. These Mittens serve just that purpose and, aside from protests, can cover a multitude of bad news days. Plus they're really handy when you're on the move and need your fingers to make a gesture, which will express your feelings… er… more explicitly.

Knitted in the round in contrast colours, with duplicate stitch lettering.

DIFFICULTY LEVEL: MEDIUM

MATERIALS

Cascade Longwood Sport (100% Merino Wool, 100g/250m/273yds) as follows:

■ 1 x 100g ball in shade #30 (Silver Heather) (A)
■ 1 x 100g ball in shade #45 (Orange) (B)
■ 1 x 100g ball in shade #21 (Blue) (C)
4 x 3.75mm (US 5) dpns
4 x press studs
2 x St-holders
Darning needle (for duplicate st lettering)

TENSION/GAUGE

24 sts and 32 rows = 10cm (4") over St-st (after blocking)

SIZE

20cm (8") circumference (measured around palm) / 30cm (11") cast-on edge to tip

Keep your filthy laws off my silky drawers

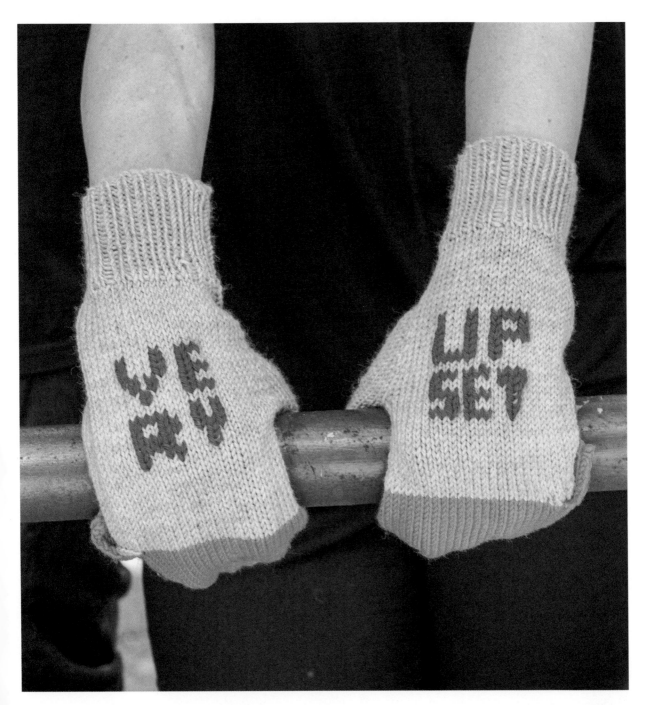

CHART 1: RIGHT MITTEN

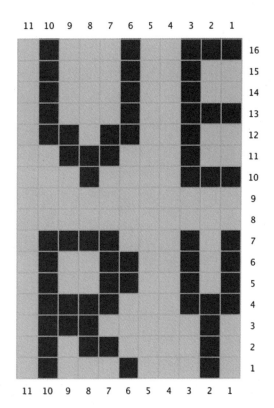

CHART 2: LEFT MITTEN

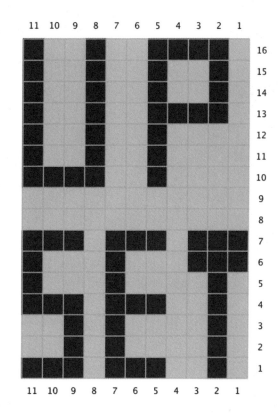

INSTRUCTIONS

Right-hand Mitten

Using A, cast on 42 sts and distribute evenly over 3 dpns (14 sts on each). Join to work in the rnd, ensuring there are no twists and PM. Work 9cm (3½") in (k1, p1) rib. **Next rnd:** (K2, kfb) 4 times, k18, (k2, kfb) 4 times. (50 sts) **Next 5 rnds:** K to end of rnd. Start thumb gusset. **Rnd 1:** Kfb, k1, kfb, PM, k to end of rnd. (52 sts) **Rnd 2 (and every even-numbered rnd):** K to end of rnd. **Rnd 3:** Kfb, k to 1 st before marker, kfb, sm, k to end of rnd. (2 sts inc) **Rnds 5-17:** Rep Rnds 2-3 seven more times. (68 sts) **Rnds 18-23:** K to end of rnd. **Rnd 24:** K1, sl next 19 sts on st-holder for Thumb, cast on 2 sts across base of Thumb, k to end of rnd. (51 sts) Divide evenly over 3 dpns (17 sts on each.) **Rnds 25-35:** K to end of rnd.* Rnd 36: K1, work 25 sts in (k1, p1) rib, turn. Working back and forth only on the last 25 sts, work 2 rows in (k1, p1) rib. Cast off for palm opening. Break yarn and re-join to rem Mitten sts, k to end of rnd. (26 sts) Put the Mitten to one side, keeping rem sts on 2 dpns.

Flap: Using 2 x 4mm dpns and B, cast on 25 sts. Work 8 rows in (k1, p1) rib. Place sts onto a st-holder. ** Return to Mitten and, using B and dpns, work as follows: with 1st needle, k1, then with same needle k15 Flap sts from st-holder; with 2nd needle, k rem 10 Flap sts from st-holder, k8 sts from Mitten; with 3rd needle, k rem 17 sts from Mitten, PM. (51 sts) K2tog at beginning of next rnd, then work in St-st (k every rnd) until Flap measures 7.5cm (3") measured from Flap cast-on rib edge. (50 sts)

Shape Top: Rnd 1: (K8, k2tog) to end of rnd. (45 sts) **Rnd 2 (and every even-numbered rnd):** K to end of rnd. **Rnd 3:** (K7, k2tog) to end of rnd. (40 sts) **Rnd 5:** (K6, k2tog) to end of rnd. (35 sts) **Rnd 7:** (K5, k2tog) to end of rnd. (30 sts) **Rnd 9:** (K4, k2tog) to end of rnd. (25 sts) **Rnd 11:** (K3, k2tog) to end of rnd. (20 sts) **Rnd 13:** (K2, k2tog) to end of rnd. (15 sts) **Rnd 15:** (K1, k2tog) to end of rnd. (10 sts)

Break yarn, leaving a long tail. Thread tail through rem 10 sts and draw up tight. Secure yarn.

Thumb: Transfer thumb sts from st-holder to dpns. Join in B, k19 thumb sts, then pick up 3 sts over base of thumb on main mitten, PM. (22 sts) Arrange sts over 3 dpns (7/8/7). Work on St-st until thumb measures 5cm (2") or desired length measured from base of thumb. **Next rnd:** (K1, k2tog) to last st, k1. (15 sts) **Next rnd:** K. **Next rnd:** (K1, k2tog) to end of rnd. (10 sts) Break off yarn, leaving a long tail. Thread tail through rem 10 sts and draw up tight. Secure yarn.

Left-hand Mitten

Follow instructions for Right-Hand Mitten to * (ending on Rnd 35), then work as follows: **Rnd 36:** K26, work 25 sts in (k1, p1) rib, turn. Now follow instructions for Flap until **. Return to Mitten and using B and dpns, work as follows: with 1st needle, k17 sts from Mitten; with 2nd needle, k rem 8 sts from Mitten, k10 Flap sts from st-holder; with 3rd needle, k rem 15 Flap sts from st-holder, k 1 st from Mitten, PM. (51 sts) K2tog at beginning of next rnd, then work in St-st (k every rnd) until Flap measures 7.5cm (3") measured from Flap cast-on rib edge. (50 sts) Shape Flap top and work Thumb following instructions for Right-Hand Mitten.

FINISHING

Lettering

For both Mittens: Working from RS on top of mittens (hand side), with flap facing towards you, count in 5 sts from Thumb, and 14 rows up from colour change, place a pin. Using C and darning needle, work duplicate st lettering from Chart 1 (Right-Hand Mitten) and Chart 2 (Left-Hand Mitten). Turn mittens inside out so that WS is facing. Press lightly using a warm iron over a damp cloth. Darn in ends.

Traffic Cone Sleeve

We shall overcone!

The joy of a graffiti knit is the element of surprise, so it needs to be quick to install and easy to remove (ensuring no long-term damage or hazards). Enter the ubiquitous traffic cone. It's not the most beautiful of things; fancy giving one a makeover? As students long ago discovered, they're just crying out to be messed with… This project gives them a pun-tastic twist with a deeper message.

This cone sleeve is straightforward to knit on two needles with a bit of colourwork and velcro sides to fit.

DIFFICULTY LEVEL: MEDIUM

MATERIALS

Patons Fairytale Fab 4-ply (100% Acrylic, 50g/184m/201yds) as follows:

☐ 1 x 50g ball in shade #1001 (White) (A)

■ 1 x 50g ball in shade #1030 (Red) (B)

■ 1 x 50g ball in shade #1099 (Black) (C)

3.25mm (US 3) needles

18cm (7") strip of velcro

The oceans are rising and so are we

TENSION/GAUGE

30 sts and 40 rows = 10cm (4") over St-st (after blocking)

SIZE

20cm (8") (h) x 35.5cm (14") (w) (measured at base) / 24cm (9½") (w) (measured at top)

NOTES

The sleeve is worked mainly in St-st with 5 moss-sts at beginning and end of each row, and 5 rows of moss-st at cast-on and cast-off edges. The shaping is worked every 8th row.

INSTRUCTIONS

Using 3.25mm circular needle and B, cast on 107 sts.
Rows 1-5: Work 5 rows in moss-st. Break B. **Row 6 (RS):** Using A, work 5 sts in moss-st, k to last 5 sts, work 5 sts in moss-st. **Row 7:** Work 5 sts in moss-st, p to last 5 sts, work 5 sts in moss-st. **Row 8 (dec row):** Work 5 sts in moss-st, k21, k2tog, k1, k2tog, k45, k2tog, k1, k2tog, k21, work 5 sts in moss-st. (103 sts) **Row 9:** Work 5 sts in moss-st, p to last 5 sts, work 5 sts in moss-st. **Row 10:** Work 5 sts in moss-st, k to last 5 sts, work 5 sts in moss-st. **Row 11:** Work 5 sts in moss-st, p24, using A, B and C, work 45 sts from chart, p to last 5 sts, work 5 sts in moss-st. **Row 12:** Work 5 sts in moss-st, k24, work 45 sts from chart, k to last 5 sts, work 5 sts in moss-st. **Rows 13-14:** Rep Rows 11-12. **Row 15:** Rep Row 11. **Row 16 (dec row):** Work 5 sts in moss-st, k20, k2tog, k1, k2tog, k 43 sts from chart, k2tog, k1, k2tog, k20, work 5 sts in moss-st. (99 sts) **Rows 17-23:** Work even in patt as set, continuing to work chart. **Row 24 (dec row):** Work 5 sts in moss-st, k19, k2tog, k1, k2tog, k 41 from chart, k2tog, k1, k2tog, k19, work 5 sts in moss-st. (95 sts) **Rows 25-31:** Work even in patt as set, continuing to work chart. **Row 32 (dec row):** Work 5 sts in moss-st, k18, k2tog, k1, k2tog, k39 sts from chart, k2tog, k1, k2tog, k18, work 5 sts in moss-st. (91 sts) **Rows 33-39:** Work even in patt as set, continuing to work chart. **Row 40 (dec row):** Work 5 sts in moss-st, k17, k2tog, k1, k2tog, k37 sts from chart, k2tog, k1, k2tog, k17, work 5 sts in moss-st. (87 sts) **Rows 41-47:** Work even in patt as set, continuing to work chart. **Row 48 (dec row):** Work 5 sts in moss-st, k16, k2tog, k1, k2tog, k35 sts from chart, k2tog, k1, k2tog, k16, work 5 sts in moss-st. (83 sts) **Rows 49-55:** Work even in patt as set, continuing to work chart. **Row 56 (dec row):** Work 5 sts in moss-st, k15, k2tog, k1, k2tog, k33 sts from chart, k2tog, k1, k2tog, k15, work 5 sts in moss-st. (79 sts) **Rows 57-63:** Work even in patt as set, continuing to work chart. **Row 64 (dec row):** Work 5 sts in moss-st, k14, k2tog, k1, k2tog, k31 sts from chart, k2tog, k1, k2tog, k14, work 5 sts in moss-st. (75 sts) **Rows 65-67:** Work even in patt as set, continuing to work chart. **Rows 68-71:** Work even in patt as set. Break C. Using A, cont as follows: **Rows 68-71:** Work 5 sts in moss-st, work to last 5 sts in St-st, work 5 sts in moss-st. **Row 72 (dec row):** Work 5 sts in moss-st, k13, k2tog, k1, k2tog, k29, k2tog, k1, k2tog, k13, work 5 sts in moss-st. (71 sts). **Rows 73-74:** Work even in patt as set. Break A. **Rows 75-79:** Using B, work 5 rows in moss-st. Cast off.

FINISHING

Press lightly using a warm iron over a damp cloth on WS. Darn in ends. Attach velcro to each side of the sleeve. Place on convenient traffic cone and run.

CROCHET PATTERNS

That voodoo that you do. Are you haunted by dreams of sticking something sharp in the face of the current leader of the free world to break his obvious bewitchment over whoever voted for him (the only logical explanation of how he came to power)?

Well with a bit of woolly magic you can; this pincushion is a safe place to store your pins and might just be the only useful thing Donny ever did. Stab away and he might just vanish in a puff of smoke.

DIFFICULTY LEVEL: HARD

MATERIALS

Robin DK (100% Acrylic, 100g/300m/328yds) as follows:

- 1 x 100g ball in shade #0137 (Melba) (A)
- 1 x 100g ball in shade #060 (Acid Yellow) (B)
- 30cm (12") strand of very pale pink yarn (for eyes) (C)
- 30cm (12") strand of pink yarn (for mouth) (D)
- 30cm (12") strand of black yarn (for eyes) (E)

3.5mm (4/E) crochet hook

Darning needle (for weaving in ends and embroidering face)

Toy stuffing

Can't build a wall, hands too small

SIZE

Approx 9cm (3½") (t) x 5cm (2") (w)

TENSION/GAUGE: N/A

NOTES

This pincushion is made in continuous rounds, starting from the top of the head to the base, with facial features and crazy hairstyle added afterwards.

For the pincushion itself, you will need to keep the gauge quite tight throughout. This can be tricky when changing colours which you may find quite fiddly at first, so take it slowly and gently pull the yarns after every colour change so that you don't end up with any unwanted loose bits.

After Rnd 20, the pattern instructs you to add another strand of B to the one already in use. Do this by holding the new tail behind the work, doing one or two stitches in htr (hdc) with the two yarns held together (not the tail), and then pulling the tail taut and weaving it in behind the work (i.e. inside the pincushion) over the next few stitches (excluding the tentacle).

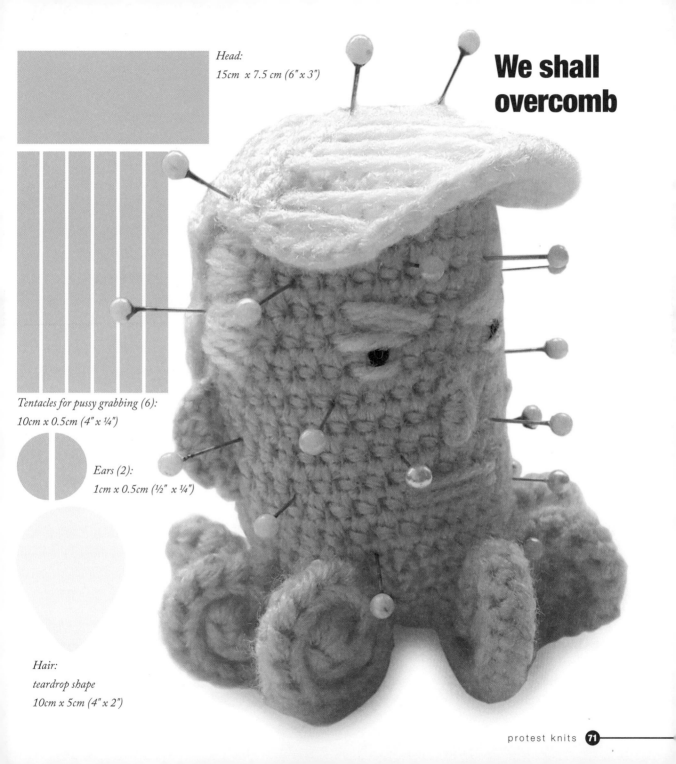

Head:
15cm x 7.5 cm (6" x 3")

We shall overcomb

Tentacles for pussy grabbing (6):
10cm x 0.5cm (4" x ¼")

Ears (2):
1cm x 0.5cm (½" x ¼")

Hair:
teardrop shape
10cm x 5cm (4" x 2")

INSTRUCTIONS

Body

Base row: Using A, make a magic ring (see Basic Techniques, p8).

Rnd 1: Make 6 htr (hdc) into circle. Pull yarn tail to tighten circle. (6 sts)

Rnd 2: Ch 2, work 2 htr (hdc) into each st, sl st into top of first st. (12 sts)

Rnd 3: Ch 2, *work 2 htr (hdc) into next st, htr (hdc) into next st; rep from * 6 times, sl st into top of first st. (18 sts)

Rnd 4: Ch 2, *work 2 htr (hdc) into next st, htr (hdc) into next 2 sts; rep from * 6 times, sl st into top of first st. (24 sts)

Rnd 5: Ch 2, *work 2 htr (hdc) into next st, htr (hdc) into next 3 sts; rep from * 6 times, sl st into top of first st. (30 sts)

Rnd 6: Ch 2, *work 2 htr (hdc) into next st, htr (hdc) into next 4 sts; rep from * 6 times, change to B, sl st into top of first st. (36 sts)

Rnd 7: Using B, ch 2, htr (hdc) into next 11 sts, change to A, then htr (hdc) into next 14 sts, change to B, then htr (hdc) into next 11 sts, sl st into top of first st.

Rnd 8: Using B, ch 2, htr (hdc) into next 11 sts, change to A, then htr (hdc) into next 15 sts, change to B, then htr (hdc) into next 10 sts, sl st into top of first st.

Rnd 9: Using B, ch 2, htr (hdc) into next 12 sts, change to A, then htr (hdc) into next 14 sts, change to B, then htr (hdc) into next 10 sts, sl st into top of first st.

Rnd 10: Using B, ch 2, htr (hdc) into next 12 sts, change to A, then htr (hdc) into next 15 sts, change to B, then htr (hdc) into next 9 sts, sl st into top of first st.

Rnd 11: Using B, ch 2, htr (hdc) into next 9 sts, change to A, then htr (hdc) into next 2 sts, change to B, then htr (hdc) into next st, change to A, then htr (hdc) into next 16 sts, change to B, then htr (hdc) into next st, change to A, then htr (hdc) into next 2 sts, change to B, then htr (hdc) into next 5 sts, sl st into top of first st.

Rnd 12: Using B, ch 2, htr (hdc) into next 9 sts, change to A, then htr (hdc) into next 23 sts, change to B, then htr (hdc) into next 4 sts, sl st into top of first st.

Rnd 13: Using B, ch 2, htr (hdc) into next 7 sts, change to A, then htr (hdc) into next 24 sts, change to B, then htr (hdc) into next 5 sts, sl st into top of first st.

Rnd 14: Using B, ch 2, htr (hdc) into next 7 sts, change to A, then htr (hdc) into next 25 sts, change to B, then htr (hdc) into next 4 sts, sl st into top of first st.

Rnd 15: Using B, ch 2, htr (hdc) into next 7 sts, change to A, then htr (hdc) into next 26 sts, change to B, then htr (hdc) into next 3 sts, change to A, sl st into top of first st.

Break B, leaving a long tail to make the eyebrows and side hair detail later. Carry B behind your work until the 11th st in the next rnd.

Using your darning needle bring the B tail out of the face on the 9th round, on the left hand side of the face as you look at it, leaving a gap of two clear holes between the last B st and your needle/yarn, which will form the left eyebrow later on.

Rnds 16-18: Using A, ch 2, htr (hdc) into each st, sl st into top of first st.

You will notice that the hairlines at the top and bottom are staggered on the back of Trump's head but don't worry about this as you will be making a crazy hairpiece later on which will cover this up.

Rnd 19: Using A, ch 1, *dec 1, htr (hdc) in next 4 sts; rep from * 6 times, sl st into top of first st. (30 sts)

Rnd 20: Ch 1, *dec 1, htr (hdc) in next 3 sts; rep from * 6 times, sl st into top of first st. (24 sts)

Add another thread of A (see Notes section), weaving in the loose end behind your work.

Tentacles

Rnd 21: Using A, ch 2, *htr (hdc) 3 times, (ch 20, turn, htr (hdc) 19 times, sl st into same st); rep from * 8 times. (24 sts)

Rnd 22: Ch 1, *dec 1, htr (hdc) in next 2 sts; rep from * 6 times. (18 sts)

Now firmly stuff the pincushion with toy stuffing.

Rnd 23: Ch 1, *dec 1, htr (hdc) in next st; rep from * 6 times. (12 sts)

Make sure the pincushion is firmly stuffed and add more toy stuffing if necessary – this design looks best with quite a fat chin.

Rnd 24: Ch 1, (dec 1) 6 times. (6 sts).

Finish with a sl st then fasten off and weave the end inside the pincushion.

Eyebrows

Using your darning needle, thread the B yarn tail which you left in position earlier into your needle. Count right 3 sts and down 1 st and insert the needle here. Go back over the eyebrow once more and then bring the yarn out again to the right of the sts just made, leaving just one stitch gap in between the two eyebrows. Count up 1 st and another 3 sts to the right, insert needle here, go over it once more and then secure by taking the needle out through the back and securing with a knot where it will not be seen (once the hairpiece is on). Then use the rest of the tail to add a few long sts of hair detail either side.

Eyes

Thread your darning needle with C and tie a knot in the end. Insert the needle in through the back of the head and pull out of the front, so that the knot gets caught up inside the pincushion. Bring the needle through 1 st down from the left end of the left eyebrow, as you face it. Count 3 sts right and insert here, then go over again. Bring the needle out again down 1 st from the left edge of the upper eyelid, count right 2

sts and go over again. Now bring the yarn through immediately to the right of the left end of the right eyebrow, along 3 sts to the right and over again. Finally, come out down 1 st from the left end of the right upper eyelid, right 2 sts, over again and secure again with a knot on the back of the pincushion.
Using D and E respectively, add the eyes and mouth.

Nose

Using A, begin with a sl st on your hook, find st between eyebrows, count 4 rows down and insert your hook into this st. Pull a loop through the nearest hole in the row above and make a dc (sc). Rep this twice more, then anchor with a sl st in the middle of the eyebrows and work back down the Nose as follows:
Into the top st, crochet a dc (sc).
Into the next st crochet a htr (hdc) and into the bottom st crochet a tr (dc).
Finish with a sl st under the base of the nose then bring the yarn out of the back of the head, securing with a knot on the back. Hide both yarn ends inside the pincushion by taking them through with the darning needle, pulling taut and trimming with scissors so that the ends pop back inside.

Ears (make 2)

Make this in the same way as the nose. Using A, begin with a sl st on your hook and insert it into the base of the ear. Make 4 vertical dcs (scs) in the ear space. Anchor with a sl st above and turn.
In the top st, work 1 dc (sc) and 1 htr (hdc); in the middle st work 2 tr (dc); in the bottom st work 1 htr (hdc) and 1 dc (sc).
Sl st at the bottom then turn and work 1 dc (sc) in each st before fastening off at the top and weaving in the tail.
Rep for the ear on the other side.

Hairpiece

The Hairpiece is crocheted in two parts, which are sewn together before being sewn onto the head.

Hair Front

Base row: Using B, make a magic ring.
Rnd 1: Ch 2, 6 htr (hdc) into ring. Pull yarn tail to tighten circle. (6 sts)
Rnd 2: Ch 2, work 2 htr (hdc) into each st, sl st into top of first st. (12 sts)
Rnd 3: Ch 2, *work 2 htr (hdc) into next st, htr (hdc) into next st; rep from * 6 times, sl st into top of first st. (18 sts)
Rnd 4: Ch 2, *work 2 htr (hdc) into next st, htr (hdc) into next 2 sts; rep from * 6 times, sl st into top of first st. (24 sts)
Rnd 5: Ch 2, *work 2 htr (hdc) into next st, htr (hdc) into next 3 sts; rep from * 6 times, sl st into top of first st. (30 sts)
Rnd 6: Ch 2, *work 2 htr (hdc) into next st, htr (hdc) into next 4 sts; rep from * 6 times, sl st into top of first st. (36 sts)
Rnd 7: Ch 2, *work 2 htr (hdc) into next st, htr (hdc) into next 5 sts; rep from * 6 times, sl st into top of first st. (42 sts)
Finish with a sl st and fasten off, leaving a long tail for sewing.

Hair Back

Base row: Using B, ch 16. (16 sts)
Rows 2-13: Ch 3, work 1 htr (hdc) in each st, turn. Fasten off, leaving a long tail for sewing.
Now sew the two parts together using one of the long tails. Place the hairpiece on top of your pincushion (with the original tail from the centre of the circle on the underside). Use pins to hold it in position while you sew it to the head along the back and sides using the other long tail. Use a tacking stitch), so that most of the stitches are hidden. Finally, using whichever of the yellow tails is longest, add a few stitches to the hairpiece.
Fasten off, darn in ends. Stab with abandon.

Park with Pride with this comfortable saddle cover. Start at the bottom (literally) and work your way up by addressing two important questions: why should we be told who we're supposed to love? And why should bike saddles be boring? Bikes are also the perfect way to get around – carbon-neutral, healthy, traffic-dodging – so you can feel righteous from bottom to top.

Easily crocheted in dc (sc) for a standard-sized saddle (you could adapt the pattern to your own size saddle).

DIFFICULTY LEVEL: EASY

MATERIALS

DMC Natura Just Cotton (100% Cotton, 50g/155m/169yds) as follows:

- 1 x 50g ball in shade #23 (Passion) (A)
- 1 x 50g ball in shade #47 (Safran) (B)
- 1 x 50g ball in shade #83 (Ble) (C)
- 1 x 50g ball in shade #13 (Pistache) (D)
- 1 x 50g ball in shade #80 (Salome) (E)
- 1 x 50g ball in shade #59 (Prune) (F)

3mm (D/3) crochet hook

TENSION/GAUGE

22 sts and 21 rows = 10cm (4") over dc (sc)

SIZE

23cm (9") (l) x 18cm (7") (w) (measured at widest point) x 3cm (1¼") (w) (measured at narrowest point) x 6.5cm (2½") (t)

Still here, still queer

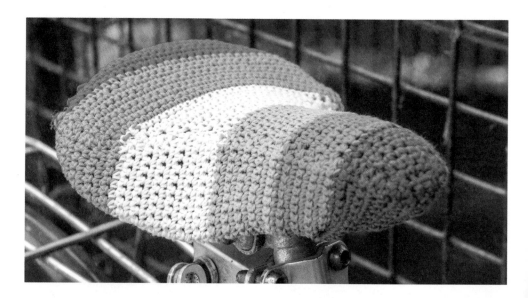

NOTES

This cover is designed to fit a commonly-available, average-size saddle, but do check the measurements and shape of your own saddle before making. The width of the sides can be adjusted by making a base chain of fewer or more sts. Alternatively, you can draw out a template of your saddle and decrease/increase sts according to the required shape.

INSTRUCTIONS

Main Saddle

Base row: Using A, ch 16, turn. (16 sts) **Row 1 (RS):** Ch 3, dc (sc) into 2nd and 3rd ch from hook, work dc (sc) to end of row, turn. (18 sts) **Rows 2-8:** Rep Row 1. (32 sts) Break A, change to B. **Rows 9-10:** Rep Row 1. (36 sts) **Rows 11-14:** Ch 1, work dc (sc) to end of row, turn. **Row 15:** Ch 1, dec 1, work dc (sc) to last 2 sts, dec 1, turn. (34 sts) **Row 16:** Rep Row 15. (32 sts) Break B, change to C. **Row 17:** Ch 1, dec 2, work dc (sc) to last 4 sts, dec 2, turn. (28 sts) **Rows 18-19:** Rep Row 17. (20 sts) **Row 20:** Ch 1, dec 1, work dc (sc) to last 2 sts, dec 1, turn. (18 sts) **Rows 21-23:** Rep Row 20. (12 sts) **Row 24:** Work dc (sc) to end of row, turn. Break C, change to D. **Row 25:** Ch 1, work dc (sc) to end of row, turn. **Row 26:** Ch 1, dec 1, work dc (sc) to last 2 sts, dec 1, turn. (10 sts) **Rows 27-32:** Ch 1, work dc (sc) to end of row, turn. Break D, change to E. **Rows 33-37:** Ch 1, work dc (sc) to end of row, turn. **Row 38:** Ch 1, dec 1, work dc (sc) to last 2 sts, dec 1, turn. (8 sts) Break E, change to F. **Row 39:** Ch 1, work dc (sc) to end of row, turn. **Row 40:** Ch 1, dec 1, work dc (sc) to last 2 sts, dec 1, turn. (6 sts) **Rows 41-44:** Ch 1, work dc (sc) to end of row, turn. **Rows 45-46:** Ch 1, dec 1, work dc (sc) to last 2 sts, dec 1, turn. (2 sts) Break yarn, thread tail through last st and tighten.

Sides (one piece)

Base row: Using A, ch 12, turn. Using A, work 20 rows in dc (sc) (remembering to work 1 turning ch at the start of each row). Break A. Throughout this section, ch 1 at the beginning of each row (for turning ch). Change to B, work 10 rows in dc (sc). Break B. Change to C, work 13 rows in dc (sc). Break C. Change to D, work 10 rows in dc (sc). Break D. Change to E, work 8 rows in dc (sc). Break E. Change to F, work 20 rows in dc (sc). Break F. Change to E, work 8 rows in dc (sc). Break E. Change to D, work 10 rows in dc (sc). Break D. Change to C, work 13 rows in dc (sc). Break C. Change to B, work 10 rows in dc (sc). Break B. Change to A, work 20 rows in dc (sc). Break yarn, thread tail through last st and tighten.

FINISHING

Press lightly using a warm iron over a damp cloth on WS. Darn in ends. Pin Sides to the Main Saddle, ensuring you match up corresponding colours. Attach Sides to the Main Saddle using dc (sc) in appropriate colours. Sew the two edges together at the back. Run a gathering st around the bottom edge of the Sides. Fit the cover over your bike saddle, tighten and secure the gathering st to fit. Pedal like fury.

Down with bad stuff

Meet metal with petal and spread the love with these quick-to-crochet flowers. We've all seen the classic images of flowers being placed down the barrel of a gun, right? Guaranteed to diffuse any aggressive situation – you could crochet these on the go and you might even raise a smile.

Incredibly quick and easy to crochet using basic crochet stitches – good stash busters.

DIFFICULTY LEVEL: EASY

MATERIALS

DMC Natura Just Cotton (100% Cotton, 50g/155m/169yds) as follows:

■ 1 x 50g ball in shade #13 (Pistache) (A)

□ 1 x 50g ball in shade #83 (Ble) (B)

Different petal shades used in photo:

□ 1 x 50g ball in shade #01 (Ibiza) (C1)

■ 1 x 50g ball in shade #47 (Safran) (C2)

■ 1 x 50g ball in shade #59 (Prune) (C3)

(If you prefer to use scraps from your stash, you will need approx 25g per flower)

3mm (D/3) crochet hook

SIZE

Flower diameter: 4cm (1½"); Stem length: 5cm (2")

FINISHING

Sew Sepals to base of Flower. Darn in ends. Spread the love.

INSTRUCTIONS

Main Flower

Using B, make a magic ring (see Basic Techniques, p8). **Rnd 1:** Ch 1, work 10 dc (sc) into circle, pull yarn tail to tighten circle, turn. **Rnd 2:** Ch 1, 1 dc (sc) in each dc (sc) to end, sl st into top of first dc (sc), turn. Break yarn and join in C (dependent on which colour you wish to use). **Rnd 3:** Ch 2, *5 tr (dc) into next dc (sc), sl st into next dc (sc); rep from * to end. Break yarn.

Sepals and Stem

For Sepals: Using A only, rep instructions for Main Flower. Break yarn. For Stem: Insert hook into the centre of the bottom of the Sepals, and hook into a st. Wrap yarn around the hook and pull through to secure the Stem to the bottom of the flower. Work 12 ch, then work sl st into each ch back along the row. Sl st into the base of the Sepals to secure. Break yarn.

Haven't you had enough already of all this talk of walls? When did they ever solve any problems? We may be living in the digital age, but print is far from dead and leaflets are still an effective way of spreading the word. Carry yours comfortably in this bold crochet bag and spread the word.

Crocheted in dc (sc), our version uses a leather strap to give it extra strength.

DIFFICULTY LEVEL: MEDIUM

MATERIALS

DMC Natura Just Cotton (100% Cotton 50g/155m/169yds) as follows:

■ 4 x 50g balls in shade #23 (Passion) (A)

☐ 4 x 50g balls in shade #02 (Ivory) (B)

3mm (C/2) crochet hook

1 x leather bag strap (shown with a 19mm (0.75") wide/119cm (47") long leather strap)

0.5 m (½ yd) lining material

TENSION/GAUGE

22 sts and 24 rows = 10cm (4") over dc (sc)

SIZE

Main Bag: 33cm (13") (w) x 25cm (10") (h) x 3.75cm (1½") (d)

Flap: 33cm (13") (w) x 7.5cm (3") (d)

Build bridges
not walls

CHART 1

CHART 2

INSTRUCTIONS

Outer front, back, flap panels (make 2)

With A, make 136 ch (inc 1 turning ch), turn. Commencing with second st from hook, work in dc (sc) as follows: Using A, work 6 rows in dc (sc). Change to B, work 6 rows. Change to A, work 6 rows. Break yarn and finish off last st.

Central front, back, flap panels (worked in one piece)

Front section: Using A, make 40 ch (inc 1 turning ch), turn. Commencing with second st from hook, work in dc (sc) as follows: Using A, work 15 rows. Work Chart A over next 45 rows, using A and B, ensuring that you work 1 turning ch at beginning of each row (not included in chart).

Bottom section: Using A, work 9 rows.

Back section: Continuing in A, work 15 rows. Change to B, work 15 rows. Rep last 30 rows once.

Top section: Change to A, work 9 rows.

Flap section: Change to B, work 15 rows. Work Chart B over next 15 rows using A and B, ensuring that you work 1 turning ch at the beginning of each row (not included in chart). Break yarn and finish off last st.

Sides (make 2)

Using A, 56 ch (inc 1 turning ch), turn. Commencing with second st from hook, work in dc (sc) as follows: Using A, work 9 rows. Break yarn and finish off last st.

FINISHING

With WS facing, attach the two Outer Panels to either side of the Central Panel (either using sewing or sl st), being sure to align the front, bottom and back sections to the correct edges of the flap. Place the work on top of your lining fabric and mark out the outline, adding an extra 2cm (¾") for seam allowance. Do the same for the two Sides and put to one side. Fold the bag according to the different sections (i.e., Front, Bottom, Back and Flap). Pin in place. Using either sewing or sl st, attach the long edges of one of the Sides to the Front and Back of the main bag, and the short edge to the bottom to form an oblong box. Rep for the second side. Attach the leather strap to the top of the Sides. Darn in ends.

Return to your lining fabric:

With WS facing, fold over and sew a 2cm (¾") hem at the top and bottom of the long strip of main bag fabric. Fold over and sew a 2cm (¾") hem at the top of the sides. Rep sewing instructions as per the main crochet bag and press using a warm iron. With the lining still inside out, place it inside the main crochet bag and secure by stitching carefully around the top edges, making sure your stitches aren't visible on the RS.

Tree Hugger Scarf

Your trees need yew

Trees: living, breathing, earth-saving organisms. So why the hell are we chopping them down? To protest against this insanity, you could a) climb one and refuse to come down, b) form a human chain around the trunk with your mates, or c) crochet this handy scarf and wrap it round a trunk to symbolise your unity with these arboreal wonders. Also doubles up as a handy bit of graffiti knit if you can bear to part with it.

Crocheted in one piece, the hands are knitted in dc (sc), with cuffs made in tr (hdc) and the main scarf in a simple shell stitch.

DIFFICULTY LEVEL: HARD

MATERIALS

DMC Natura Just Cotton (100% Cotton, 50g/155m/169yds) as follows:

■ 3 x 50g balls in shade #64 (Prusian) (A)

☐ 1 x 50g ball in shade #02 (Ivory) (B)

▨ 1 x 50g ball in shade #80 (Salome) (C)

3mm (D/3) crochet hook

TENSION/GAUGE

22 sts and 21 rows = 10cm (4") over dc (sc)

SIZE

170cm (67") (l) (measured from fingertips)
x 14.5cm (5¾") (w) (width of main scarf)

There is no Planet B

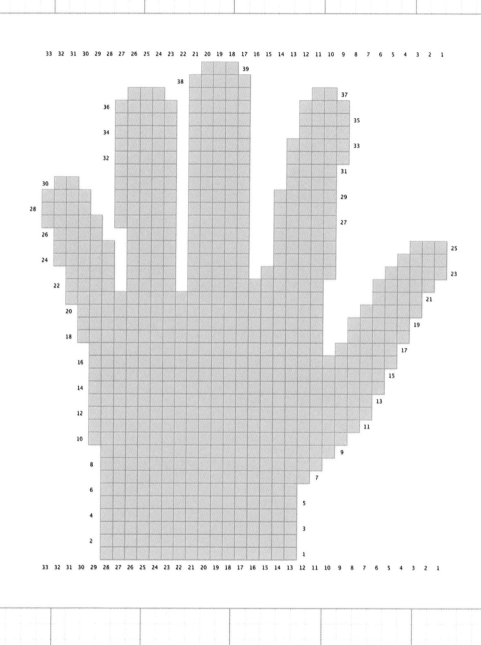

INSTRUCTIONS

Right Hand

Base row: Using C, ch 16. (16 sts) **Rows 1-39:** Ch 1, work 39 rows from chart in dc (sc), decreasing and increasing where indicated for shaping. Throughout this section, ch 1 at the beginning of each row (for turning ch). Work chart until you reach the point where the thumb separates from the palm (Row 16). Work thumb, then break yarn and re-join to the main palm. Work main palm rows as indicated, then work index finger. Break yarn and rejoin to the main palm to work the middle finger. Cont in this fashion until all fingers have been worked. Break yarn.

Cuff, Main Scarf, Left Hand (worked in one piece)

Place Hand with fingers facing towards you and thumb pointing to the left.

Cuff: Row 1 (RS): Using B, ch 3, then work 16 tr (dc) (one into each of the 16 dc (sc) of the Hand Base Row), turn. (16 sts) **Row 2:** Ch 3, inc 1 st into each tr (dc), turn. (32 sts) **Row 3:** Ch 3, *inc 1, tr (dc) 3); rep from * to end, turn. (40 sts) Break B.

Main Scarf: Using A, work patt as follows: **Base row (WS):** Ch 3, work 2 tr (dc) into 1st tr (dc), *skip 2 tr (dc), 1 dc (sc) into next tr (dc), skip 2 tr (dc), 5 tr (dc) into next tr (dc); rep from * 6 times to end of row, ending with skip 2 tr (dc), 1 dc (sc) into last tr (dc), turn. **Row 1:** Ch 3, 2 tr (dc) into dc (sc), *1 dc (sc) in centre (3rd st) of tr (dc) group, 5 tr (dc) in dc (sc); rep from * to end of row ending with 1 dc (sc) into top of turning ch, turn. Rep Row 1 until Main Scarf measures 135cm (53") (or desired length) measured from base of Cuff and finishing with a RS row. Break A.

Cuff: Row 1 (WS): Using B, ch 3, *dec 1, tr (dc) 3; rep from * to end, turn. (32 sts) **Row 2:** Ch 3, dec 1 st to end, turn. (16 sts) **Row 3:** Ch 3, work one row tr (dc). (16 sts) Break B.

Left Hand

Rows 1-39: Using C, ch 1, work 39 rows from chart in dc (sc), decreasing and increasing where indicated for shaping and remembering to ch 1 for turning ch at the beginning of each row (see Basic Techniques, p8). Break yarn.

FINISHING

With WS facing, press lightly using a warm iron over a damp cloth. Darn in ends.

Hand Outline

Using C, work a sl st into the base of one of the Hands, then proceed to work in dc (sc) around the outside of the Hand. When you work the tips of each finger, work as follows: 3 dc (sc) into 1 st, work either 3 dc (sc) (for thumb, middle and ring fingers) or 2 dc (sc) (for index and little fingers) into tip of finger, 3 dc (sc) into 1 st, cont down the other side of finger using dc (sc) only as before. When you reach the joint between two fingers: dec 1 st into the base of the finger, then cont up the side of the next finger. At the end of the hand outline, finish with a sl st, break yarn. Rep for second hand. Darn in ends.

Make Earth cool again

Acknowledgements

A big heartfelt thanks as ever to Roger and Lucas for your support and for sharing me with my needles and yarn. As every knitting author knows, your patterns are only as good as your editor and Gwendolyn Wagner-Adair is as good as they get – thanks Gwen for your knowledge, patience and incredible attention to detail.

Thanks too to knitters and crocheters Annie Christopher, Jean Luff and Caroline Bletsis who helped me bring some of these creations to life, and to Kat Stiff for her design, the incredible Trump Voodoo Pincushion. Very grateful to that most excellent photographer Ivan Jones who brought the book to life with his humour and lens skills; speaking of which, a big hearty cheers to that rent-a-gang of protestors, David Samuel, Josh Samuel-Gaitens, Vicky Barnard, Joanna Copperman, Lara Murphy, John Conlon and Madeline Meckiffe featured in the crowd scenes in the book; and to all at Plum5 for their hard work.

The flask holder project was inspired by the passionate activist Marina Pepper who you will find at protests helping both protestors and those in positions of authority to feel safe and comfortable by handing out tea, poured out of a china teapot into china cups.

Final credit goes to all those brilliant knitting revolutionaries who just won't give up –

keep knitting and keep fighting!

Photographic credits: All photographs © Shutterstock unless otherwise stated.

Photographs by Ivan Jones: pages 18, 19, 21, 23, 27, 28, 31, 34, 35, 37, 39, 42, 43, 47, 50, 51, 56-57, 59, 62, 63, 65, 68-69, 78, 80, 82, 83, 84-85, 87, 89, 92, 93

Alamy: pages 24-25, 40-41

Trump pincushion courtesy of Katrina Stiff, Snorkers Imaginarium

Charts by Gwendolyn Wagner-Adair